HOW? WHO? WHAT? WHEN? WHERE? WHY?

Questions
kids
ask

ABOUT
PLANTS

PUBLISHER	Joseph R. DeVarennes	
PUBLICATION DIRECTOR	Kenneth H. Pearson	
ADVISORS	Roger Aubin	
	Robert Furlonger	
EDITORIAL SUPERVISOR	Jocelyn Smyth	
PRODUCTION MANAGER	Ernest Homewood	
PRODUCTION ASSISTANTS	Martine Gingras	Kathy Kishimoto
	Catherine Gordon	Peter Thomlison
CONTRIBUTORS	Alison Dickie	Nancy Prasad
	Bill Ivy	Lois Rock
	Jacqueline Kendel	Merebeth Switzer
	Anne Langdon	Dave Taylor
	Sheila Macdonald	Alison Tharen
	Susan Marshall	Donna Thomson
	Pamela Martin	Pam Young
	Colin McCance	
SENIOR EDITOR	Robin Rivers	
EDITORS	Brian Cross	Ann Martin
	Anne Louise Mahoney	Mayta Tannenbaum
PUBLICATION ADMINISTRATOR	Anna Good	
ART AND DESIGN	Richard Comely	Marilyn Mets
	George Elliott	Ronald Migliore
	Greg Elliott	Sue Wilkinson

Canadian Cataloguing in Publication Data

Main entry under title

Questions kids ask about plants

(Questions kids ask ; 9)
ISBN 0-7172-2548-8

1. Plants—Miscellanea—Juvenile literature.
2. Children's questions and answers.
I. Smyth, Jocelyn.   II. Comely, Richard.   III. Series.

QK49.Q84 1988   j581   C89-093068-6

Questions Kids Ask . . . about PLANTS

continued

How many plants are there in the world?

If you ever start out to make a list of all the plants in the world, make sure you have a lot of time and a lot of paper! Why? Because there are over 350 000 different species of plants worldwide.

Plants can be found in water, on land and in the air, in fact just about anywhere the moisture and temperature are suitable. Some plants, such as one-celled bacteria and algae, are so small you need a microscope to see them. Others, like certain species of trees, can weigh as much as 2000 metric tons.

The majority of plants bear flowers, many of which are very beautiful. Think how drab this world would be without them!

Do bananas grow on trees?

Everybody loves a delicious banana split. Bananas are so tasty and nutritious they have been a favorite fruit for hundreds of years. Have you every wondered where bananas come from?

Bananas grow in tropical countries where the temperature is hot all year round. They grow on plants that are so large that people often mistake them for trees. A banana plant is not a tree. It is an herb! The large "trunk" is actually a long leaf-covered stalk that grows straight up out of the ground. Great yellow flowers sprout from the top of the false trunk and eventually produce large bunches of bananas. As many as 150 bananas may grow from a single stalk!

What is an eggplant?

No, it's not a plant that grows eggs! It's called that because some varieties of eggplant have smooth, egg-shaped fruit. Other names for it are aubergine and garden egg. While eggplants con

What is a coconut?

Coconuts are the large round fruit of the coconut-palm. They grow in clusters high up in the tree. The seed—the part that's good for eating—is locked up tight within two thick outside layers called the rind and the husk. These are usually cut away before marketing. The husk can be woven into mats, ropes and even brooms. The seed is further protected by a hard brown shell. This must be split open to get the two delicious treats inside: the sweet white coconut meat that sticks to the shell and a white watery liquid called coconut milk. Solid, dried coconut meat is called copra and contains a valuable oil used in cooking, margarine and soap production. Tropical lands export huge quantities of copra every year.

Seven or eight years after a coconut palm is planted it begins to produce coconuts. It takes about a year for each coconut to ripen and a healthy tree can produce as many as 50 each year.

in white, brown and yellow, the light and deep purple ones are the best for eating.

DID YOU KNOW . . . long ago people believed eggplants were poisonous!

Eggplant can be prepared in many tasty ways, and has been eaten for centuries in the East. However, it doesn't contain many vitamins or calories.

The fruit of the eggplant can be anywhere from the size of a plum to the size of a football and the plant itself can grow up to 2 metres (6 feet) tall. It grows only in warm weather and takes from 115 to 120 days to ripen.

7

How long can a cactus live without water?

A cactus can go without water for months—much longer than any other plant—because it's very good at living in dry regions.

Most cacti are found in North America, in the southern United States and Mexico. There are over 1500 different kinds—and all of them live without much water. In fact, too much water can kill them.

It may not rain for months in the desert, but it does rain occasionally. In order to take full advantage of the rain when it comes, cacti keep their roots close to the surface of the ground. That way, they'll be sure to catch the rainwater as it trickles down.

Rather than leaves, cacti grow prickly spines, and less water is able to escape through them.

A cactus stores water in its spongy or hollow stem, which is where it makes its food too. The outer layer is thick and waxy and this also prevents water from escaping. All these special cactus tricks have taken thousands of generations to perfect.

Are cacti useful?

Yes, cacti are useful. As long as you learn to respect a cactus's sharp spines, you'll find that they come in handy in all sorts of ways.

Just ask the Indians of Arizona who use the dried stems of the Saguaro cactus to make buildings and for fuel. They also eat its fruit, which ripens in June, and then save the rest by making preserves. The seeds of some cacti are ground and used in making cakes. The barrel cactus is an important source of fresh water in the desert. People in some parts of Mexico boil or fry part of the Opuntia cactus. They also cook the flowers and fruit and use them in salads.

DID YOU KNOW . . . woodpeckers and tiny owls live in holes in large Saguaro cacti where they are safe from most enemies.

Why is a cactus prickly?

Grabbing a cactus is like holding a fistful of sharp needles. Ouch! Cactus plants are covered with sharp bristles that prick and scratch if you touch them. The prickly bristles are called spines.

Like animals, some species of plants have developed special features that help them protect themselves. A cactus's sharp spines do this by discouraging plant-eating animals. One chomp on a cactus, and the hungry animal ends up with a mouthful of prickles. Few ask for a second helping.

The spines also help cacti survive the dry, hot climate most of them grow in because they don't give off water as leaves would.

Could we live without plants?

Plants not only add color and beauty to our world, but our very life depends on them.

Wood, rubber, paper, cotton and medicine are just a few of the products plants provide us with. One can, of course, imagine life going on without those things—but plants also supply us with two necessities of life: food and oxygen.

You might think that we could get by without plants by living on meat. We couldn't, though, because all animals depend on plants for nourishment. Even those that do not eat plants themselves feed on animals that do. Therefore if all the plants in the world were to die, every living creature—including us—would starve.

And if there were any way around *that* problem, we would not be much better off because we would all suffocate. People and animals breathe in oxygen from the air and exhale carbon dioxide. Plants, on the other hand, take in carbon dioxide and give off oxygen. In this way they prevent the world's vital supply of oxygen from running out.

Are all plants green?

Not all plants are green, but most of them are. They are green because they produce a very important substance called chlorophyll. Chlorophyll is made up of several colors, with green usually dominating.

Chlorophyll is used for photosynthesis, a process by which green plants use the energy of sunlight to change water and carbon dioxide into the food they need to grow.

Which plants aren't green? Mainly those that don't contain chlorophyll, such as mushrooms and other fungi. Without chlorophyll, these plants can't produce food and must get it from other plant and animal materials.

DID YOU KNOW . . . not all plants that contain chlorophyll are green. In some—mainly algae —other pigments such as brown, red and yellow mask the green color of the chlorophyll.

Why do plants turn toward the light?

We do not think of plants as moving since their movements are usually too slow to be seen.

However, plants are rarely still during the day—they steadily turn toward the light. For example, any plant placed on a windowsill will lean toward the sunlight outside. This is because plant cells contain a growth substance known as auxin which moves away from light and gathers on the dark side of the stem. This causes the shaded side of the stem to grow faster and as a result the stalk bends in the direction of the light. For this reason it is a good idea to rotate houseplants so they grow evenly.

What is moss?

If you have ever been in the woods you have no doubt seen lots of moss. Thousands of these velvety green plants often form dense mats on the forest floor and cover the base of trees and rocks.

There are about 15 000 kinds of moss. Most thrive in dark, damp places where many other plants find it difficult to grow. They have thin stems and narrow leaves. Mosses have no true roots and produce neither flowers nor seeds. Instead they reproduce by means of spores.

DID YOU KNOW . . . mosses are so absorbent that some North American Indians once used these plants to diaper their babies and to dress wounds.

Does moss always grow on the north side of a tree?

According to folklore moss only grows on the north side of trees, and therefore people lost in the woods can rely on this natural compass to help them find their way out. There is some truth to this tale. Moss grows best in damp, shady places. Since bright sunshine seldom strikes the north side of trees, moss grows thickest there. However, in a dense forest, where very little sun penetrates, it often grows on all sides of a tree. For this reason moss is not a fool-proof guide and it is best to depend on a real compass when hiking in the woods.

What is a mushroom?

If you take a walk in the woods after a spell of wet weather, you'll likely see plenty of mushrooms. They look like small umbrellas and are probably the best known of the plants called fungi.

The main part of a mushroom, the mycelium, is underground. It looks like a web of tiny white threads and is both the roots and the trunk of the mushroom.

The part of the mushroom that looks like an umbrella is called the sporophore. It is the fruit of the mushroom and its job is to scatter the plant's cells so new mushroom plants can grow.

When the top, called the crown, spreads out you can see that its underside is covered with thin ridges, or gills. These make the spores, which are the cells that will float away and grow into new mushrooms.

Like all fungi, mushrooms can't make their own food, so they use the food that other plants have made. You will usually find mushrooms growing on tree stumps, logs or on the ground where there is a lot of decaying plant matter.

Have you ever heard the story that light circles of grass on a lawn or meadow were made by fairies dancing in the night? The real cause of the light grass is the mycelium of a large fungus that produces a ring of small mushrooms around it. The grass above the mycelium gets thinner than the rest of the grass, making it look as if it has been trampled by tiny feet.

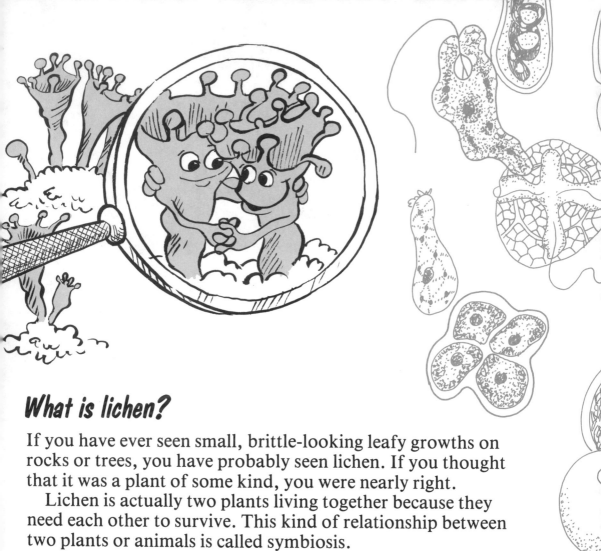

What is lichen?

If you have ever seen small, brittle-looking leafy growths on rocks or trees, you have probably seen lichen. If you thought that it was a plant of some kind, you were nearly right.

Lichen is actually two plants living together because they need each other to survive. This kind of relationship between two plants or animals is called symbiosis.

The two plants that make up lichen are a fungus and blue-green algae. You have probably seen blue-green algae in ponds, or aquariums. Green plants, like algae, contain chlorophyll, which they use to convert the energy from the sun into food. Fungi have no chlorophyll, so they must get their food from other sources. On the other hand, fungi hold moisture better than algae because of their fleshier tissues.

So lichen is a plant partnership where one plant (the fungus) keeps the other from drying out, and the other plant (the algae) supplies the food.

What are algae?

Algae are very unusual plants. They have no roots, stems or leaves, nor do they bear flowers or produce seeds. They come in all sizes and shapes. Most of the world's 25 000 different species of algae live in the water. Some are so tiny that they contain only one cell. These algae have whip-like hairs which help propel them through the water. The green slimy scum that forms on the surface of still water is actually millions of these plants grouped together. The largest algae are the seaweeds, some of which are more than 60 metres (200 feet) long.

Many sea creatures and some people who live on the coast include algae in their diet. Certain varieties are used in our foods. One species of brown algae, the seaweed kelp, provides a substance which is used to thicken ice cream and mayonnaise. Some red algae are the source of an ingredient used in candies and some dairy products.

What is the largest flower in the world?

Does this question have you skunked? Well, the largest flower in the world is that of the rafflesia, also known as the stinking corpse lily. This mottled orange-brown and white flower is found in the jungles of Southeast Asia. A single bloom can measure almost a metre (3 feet) across, have petals over two centimetres (3/4 of an inch) thick and weigh up to 11 kilograms (24 pounds).

Despite its impressive size, the rafflesia is one flower you certainly would not want to include in a bouquet. As its other name suggests, it has one of the most sickening smells in all of nature. Instead of attracting bees, this stinker draws flies.

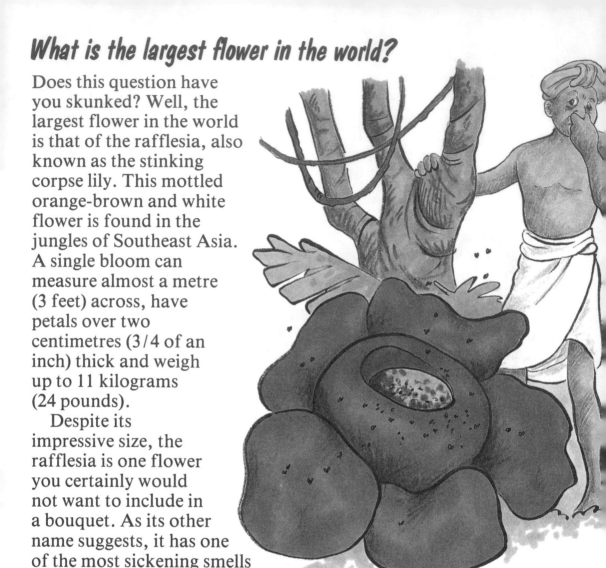

Do buttercups make your chin yellow?

If they do, it's only for the few moments that the bright yellow flower is held under your chin. If your chin reflects the yellow from the flower, that's supposed to mean you like butter.

Buttercups usually have five rounded petals and get their name from the cup-shaped blossom. They are very common and grow mostly in fields, woods and along roadsides.

Even though these flowers are pretty, neither farmers nor cattle like them much. The cows don't like them because they have a bitter, burning juice that makes them a bad snack. And because no animals will eat them, buttercups grow wherever they want. Farmers think of them as troublesome weeds that take nutrients away from more useful plants.

Why do plants have flowers?

Yum!

Although flowers can be very beautiful they are not simply for decoration. Without them many plants would not be able to reproduce. Flowers are the place where seeds are made. Inside most flowers are two main parts, the stamens and the pistil. The stamens produce a yellow powder known as pollen, which must find its way to the pistil at that or another flower's center before seeds can be produced. Insects and birds are attracted to the flowers by their fragrance, color and sweet-tasting nectar. While helping themselves to a drink they also help the plants to make seeds by carrying the pollen from flower to flower.

Why do jumping beans jump?

A bean that jumps? It's true! Jumping beans get their name because they jump and roll from side to side. Put one on a table, and it won't be long before you see it roll and jump up in the air.

The movement is caused by the larva of a moth called *Laspeyresia saltitans*. The larva lives inside the bean. When it's full-grown, the larva grasps the walls of the bean and wriggles its body. When the larva moves, the bean "jumps."

Jumping beans grow in Central and South America. North Americans sometimes call them Mexican jumping beans. People in the southwestern states call them bronco beans because they jump like a rodeo horse. But you don't have to worry about them jumping from your dinner plate. Jumping beans are not used for food.

THEY RAISED THE BAR KID ... THINK YA' CAN MAKE IT!?

Do all roots grow underground?

We usually think of plant roots as growing underground, but this is not always the case. In addition to underground roots some plants rely on external roots for extra support. For example the mangrove trees of seaside swamps have a series of long roots that grow from the sides of the trunks to the ground below. These stilt roots act as guy wires holding the plant firmly in place as the tide flows in and out. The common corn plant also has similar prop roots growing from the lower portion of its stalk.

Another familiar plant with roots above ground is the English ivy. As this creeping vine slowly works its way up a wall or tree, a number of small roots spread out from its stem and hold the plant in place.

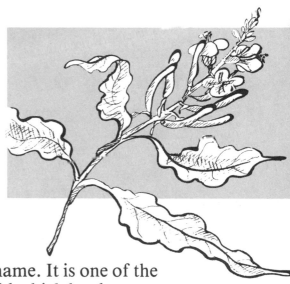

How did fireweed get its name?

It is no mystery how fireweed got its name. It is one of the first plants to grow in a forest or a field which has been burned by fire. Masses of these beautiful pink and purple spiked flowers often cover blackened land long before any other plants or trees bring color to the landscape. Since they thrive in disturbed soil they are often seen at the side of roads. These 2-metre (6-foot) tall plants bloom in the summer and are a favorite of bees. Fireweed is widespread in North America, Europe and Asia.

What happens to fallen leaves?

Each autumn millions of leaves fall to the ground. Have you ever wondered where they all go? You would think that by now we would be buried in them. Luckily, as new leaves fall on the blanket of old leaves, those below begin to decay. As they rot, molds, insects, bacteria and worms all help to break the leaves down into humus, a rich, dark substance that gradually gets mixed into the soil.

In this way, fallen leaves become part of the soil and give back the minerals and other nutrients they themselves once used. The surrounding trees use this food to grow and produce new leaves, and thus each year the cycle continues.

Why do trees have bark?

The next time you come across a tree stump, have a look inside. The trunk of a tree is divided into two main parts: a rough outer skin called the bark, and the center area called the wood.

The bumpy bark that you feel on the outside of a tree is dead. The living bark, called the phloem, lies inside the rough outer layer and is protected by it.

A tree's leaves use sunlight to produce food for the tree. This food is carried throughout the tree by the phloem. If the phloem is damaged, the tree will die.

The outer layer of dead bark helps to protect the tree from heat and cold and insect attacks.

Tree bark comes in so many different colors and textures that no two trees are exactly alike. If you have a favorite tree, spend a few minutes getting to know it by feeling its bark. Have a friend blindfold you and then try to find your tree just by the feel of its bark.

ow can trees tell us about the past?

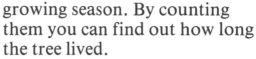

he next time you see a tree
ump, take a look at the rings.
hese are the thin lines that form
rcles inside each other on the
urface of the stump. What can
ey tell you?

They can tell you how old the
ee was when it was cut down.
ach line marks the end of a
growing season. By counting
them you can find out how long
the tree lived.

Some lines may be closer
together than others. This tells
you about the growing seasons
during the tree's life. If the lines
are far apart, there was lots of
rain and warm weather that year.
Lines that are close together
indicate a dry or short growing
season.

A few kinds of trees live for
thousands of years. Scientists
can study these trees and learn
what the weather was like
long before records were
kept. Sometimes they can use
this information to explain
mysterious historical events.

For instance, some Indian
cities were deserted hundreds
of years ago. If there are
rings close together on
ancient trees growing nearby,
scientists know that there
was a period of very dry
years. This would have
caused food crops to fail,
forcing the Indians to move
to areas where rain was
more plentiful.

How do ferns reproduce?

Very well by the looks of it. Ferns are non-flowering plants that grow in most parts of the world except for the driest deserts. They are found from the Arctic Circle to the highest mountains and most everywhere in between. Some are tiny while others grow 20 metres (65 feet) high! There are many different kinds, 10 000 species in all. Ferns reproduce by microscopic cells called spores. But there's more to the story than that.

The plant produces leaves with dots on them called sporangia. These dots burst open, releasing many tiny spores which are like seeds. One plant may produce millions of spores during a season. When spores land on the right type of ground they grow into two different types of fern—male and female. Together these new plants will produce new ferns capable of growing yet more leaves with those important dots!

What are fiddleheads?

In early spring when ferns first begin to grow, their leaves are curled into a tight coil. Since these young shoots resemble the head of a violin or fiddle, they are known as fiddleheads. Some species of fiddleheads are edible and are served as a vegetable. The fiddleheads of the ostrich fern are particularly tasty and in some areas of the world are considered a delicacy. In Canada's Maritime Provinces they are a very common dish. In Japan they are so popular that the government has passed a law to protect these wild delights from extinction.

Hi there guys!

What is the sensitive plant?

The sensitive plant, also known as *mimosa pudica* and *mimosa sensitiva,* is one of the strangest plants in the world. It is a tropical plant with fern-like leaves that bears small purplish flowers and grows about a metre (3 feet) high.

What sets the sensitive plant apart from other plants is its incredible speed of movement. Immediately after being touched, the plant responds by folding up its leaflets pair by pair. In a matter of seconds the whole leaf is closed up tight! If the touch is firm enough, the whole stalk also drops. It may take a while for this sensitive plant to recover but its leaves usually start to unfold again within fifteen minutes. The sensitive plant also reacts to light. It closes up at night, but this time with the stalks pointing up. These peculiar movements could be caused by a chemical reaction, but no one knows for sure. It is still one of the amazing mysteries of the plant world.

DID YOU KNOW . . . ferns first appeared on earth over 350 million years ago.

Do plants sleep?

Some plants do sleep, but their kind of sleep is not like ours and it happens for a different reason. Many flowers, such as the water lily and the daisy, open during the day and close at night. Other flowers, such as the evening primrose and some species of the tobacco plant, close in the day and open at night. This change in position from daytime to nighttime is called "sleep movement."

Plants do not "know" when night has come. They simply respond to the change in light or the change in temperature. Temperatures tend to fall at night.

Why do plants "sleep"? Some scientists believe that the reason is linked to insects. Insects help to move pollen from plant to plant. This allows the plants to reproduce. Those that open during the day are fertilized by insects that fly during the day. Likewise, the plants that open at night are fertilized by insects that fly during the night. Some plants close when the air is damp. Perhaps they are "sleeping" so they will keep the pollen dry!

DID YOU KNOW . . . plants are supposed to grow better when you play classical music to them.

Do plants breathe?

Just as we breathe all the time, so do plants. But plants don't have lungs and they don't take oxygen from the air the way people do. Instead, plants take in carbon dioxide from the air. It enters through tiny holes called stomata, which are found mostly in their leaves. The stomata lead to small air spaces between the cells of the leaves. Carbon dioxide traps pull the gas into the plant. Here it is made into glucose, a sugar that the plant has many uses for.

Can you guess what gas is left over after the glucose has been made? Oxygen, the gas that we need! Oxygen goes into the air spaces and out of the plant through the same stomata.

As you can see, plants and people help each other when they breathe. Humans make carbon dioxide for plants to breathe, and plants make oxygen for people to breathe.

What is a weed?

Could you plant a weed among the other flowers in your garden? No, because as soon as you plant a weed in the place you want it to grow, it is no longer a weed. A weed is a plant that grows where it is not wanted!

People usually pull up the dandelions on their lawns as soon as they see them. These plants are weeds that are spoiling the grass, the people might say. Perhaps you do not think of dandelions as weeds. If you like their pretty yellow flowers, root them up and plant them in a box of earth. Water them when they are dry and they will grow quickly. You are not growing weeds—you are growing flowers to brighten your day!

How do animals help plants?

Animals move around from place to place. Plants don't. Animals help plants by carrying seeds to new areas where they can grow.

Seeds are often carried in the stomachs of animals. When an animal eats a fruit, the seeds are carried in its stomach and then deposited in a new area with the animal's droppings. Some seeds are carried on the outside of an animal. Those nasty burrs that stick to your pants when you walk through the woods also stick to animals' fur and are one plant's method of hitching a ride.

Bees are important animals to many plants. As they move from flower to flower, bees collect plant pollen on their bodies. The pollen brushes off onto other flowers that the bee visits. The pollen that bees spread is necessary for the plants to produce seeds. Animals are the plant world's delivery people!

What is the largest living thing?

The largest living things on earth are the Giant Sequoia trees. These tall trees belong to the Redwood family of trees, which flourished 60 million years ago. Today only a few members of the family exist in North America and Japan.

The Giant Sequoia may be found only on the western slopes of the Sierra Nevada Mountains in California.

One of these trees, the General Sherman Tree, named after the famous American Civil War general, is 81 metres (267 feet) tall. It is 31 metres (102 feet) around the base. It is believed to be about 3500 years old—as old as the ancient pyramids in Egypt. This tree, found in Sequoia National Park, California, is the largest living thing on earth.

So many deliveries to make still.

What is the world's tallest grass?

The grass that grows on your lawn has many relatives including corn, wheat and rice. But would it surprise you to know that the hard, wood-like bamboo which is often used to make furniture is also a type of grass? Well it is, and it is by far the tallest.

Like lawn grass, bamboo has an underground root system

which sends up sprouts. These sprouts grow at an amazing rate. Some bamboo can reach 21 metres (70 feet) in six to eight weeks.

Some types of bamboo take 20 years to flower and others take over a century, but no matter when they flower, this is the end of the bamboo plant's life.

What is poison ivy?

Poison ivy is a very unpopular plant and if you have ever touched it you probably know why! As its name implies, it contains a poison that is so strong you can even be affected by the smoke from burning plants! The symptoms of ivy poisoning are a blistering rash and a maddening itch.

Poison ivy may grow as a vine or as a low shrub. Luckily there is an easy way to recognize it: the leaves always grow in threes. They may be glossy or dull, and have jagged or smooth edges. In early spring and in fall they are red, in the summer a deep green. The plant's small yellowish or greenish flowers are followed by waxy white berries.

About seven out of ten people are affected by poison ivy, so next time you are out in the fields or woods remember this little rhyme: "Leaves three, let them be."

What makes nettles sting?

What do bees and nettles have in common?

Believe it or not, both can give you a nasty sting. While a bee has only one stinger, nettles have hundreds! This roadside weed is covered with tiny hairs. When touched, the tip of each hollow bristle breaks off and jabs into your skin. A sac at the bottom of the hair pumps a poison into the wound that causes a painful itch. Luckily, most species of nettles are irritating but not harmful. However, a few Indonesian species can be deadly. Nettles grow as tall as 120 centimetres (4 feet), have toothed leaves and usually grow in large clusters.

What is deadly nightshade?

Deadly nightshade is another name for *belladonna,* a bushy plant that grows in Europe and Asia. The sap of the deadly nightshade was once used to make a cosmetic. That is probably how it got its other name: *belladonna* is Italian for "beautiful lady." The plant is called "deadly" because its berries contain a very strong poison and people have died from eating them.

This plant can kill you—but it can also cure you. A drug made from the plant is often used in the treatment of a variety of illnesses, including asthma, bronchitis, whooping cough, colic and serious stomach aches.

Deadly nightshade plants are sometimes grown in gardens because they are very beautiful. They grow up to one metre (3 feet) high and have bluish purple or deep red bell-shaped flowers. The poisonous berries are black. They are quite pretty to look at—but watch out! As this plant's name lets you know, eating it can cause death!

Nice garden.

I like it.

DID YOU KNOW . . . the nightshade family includes some of our favorite vegetables— eggplants, tomatoes and potatoes!

What do botanists do?

Botanists are scientists who study everything there is to know about plants, such as their growth, reproduction and diseases. They also study how plants can be used for food, medicine, dyes, wood, cloth and paper.

Plants range from one-celled bacteria to towering trees, from molds to mosses, from herbs to flowers. They are found everywhere on this planet, from the desert to the Arctic and even in the ocean. Botanists often make special trips to far-away places to study plants in their natural surroundings and to collect plant specimens to study in their laboratories.

Do plants eat meat?

Certain kinds of plants, called carnivorous plants, eat insects. These plants usually live in swampy places where they get little or no nitrogen, an important food, from the soil. In order to survive, they trap and digest insects.

There are various types of carnivorous plants. Each has a specially designed organ for trapping insects and glands that produce a juice to help it digest its food.

One group of carnivorous plants, the butterworts, have hundreds of bag-like traps on their leaves and stems. Each one has a "mouth" with tiny hairs near the opening. When an insect touches these hairs, the walls of the bag expand and suck it in. Each trap catches several insects a day!

BOTANY LAB. 14-A

NO FRED, THEY ONLY EAT INSECTS... WHY DO YOU ASK?

ow do sundews catch an insect?

.ike the butterwort, the sundew eats insects, but it has its own
nique way of catching them.

The sundew's leaves are covered with hundreds of reddish
airs, each one tipped with a drop of golden liquid. In the sun
he drops glitter like dew, which explains how the plant got its
ame. Insects are attracted to the golden liquid, mistaking it
or nectar. Too late they learn that there is a catch to this
lant! The tempting drops are as sticky as glue. When an
isect touches one it is held fast. As the victim struggles to free
self the surrounding hairs close in around it. The sundew
nen secretes an acidic fluid and the insect is slowly digested.
fter about two days the plant finishes its meal and the hairs
owly uncurl. The trap is now reset and the sundew is ready
or its next victim.

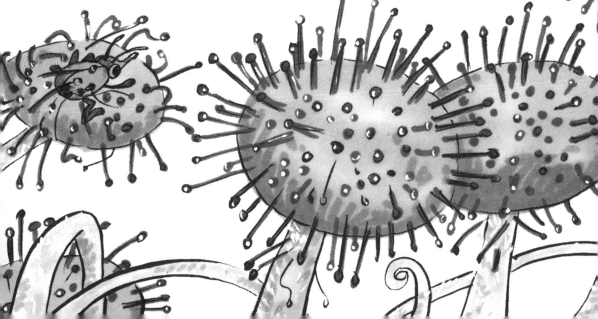

Index _____